This Book Belongs to:

Le Bon Family

Date:

2013

Saints AND Their Stories

By Maria Loretta Giraldo
Translated by Margaret Edward Moran, FSP
English adaptation by Patricia Edward Jablonski, FSP
Illustrated by Nicoletta Bertelle

Pauline
BOOKS & MEDIA
Boston

Library of Congress Cataloging-in-Publication Data

Jablonski, Patricia Edward.
  Saints and their stories / by Maria Loretta Giraldo ; translated by Margaret Edward Moran ; English adaptation by Patricia Edward Jablonski ; illustrated by Nicoletta Bertelle. -- 1st North American ed.
    p. cm.
  ISBN 0-8198-7134-6
  1. Christian saints--Biography--Juvenile literature. I. Giraldo, Maria Loretta. I Santi. English. II. Title.
  BX4653.J33 2010
  270.092'2--dc22
  [B]
                                    2010001499

The Scripture quotations contained herein are from the *New Revised Standard Version Bible: Catholic Edition*, copyright © 1989, 1993, Division of Christian Education of the National Council of the Churches of Christ in the United States of America. Used by permission. All rights reserved.

Originally published in Italian as *I santi: I miei primi amici* by Edizioni San Paolo s.r.l., Cinisello Balsamo, Milan, Italy

Published by Pauline Books & Media, 50 Saint Pauls Avenue, Boston, MA 02130-3491

Printed in Korea

STS SIPSKOGUNKYO04-10006 7134-6

www.pauline.org

Pauline Books & Media is the publishing house of the Daughters of St. Paul, an international congregation of women religious serving the Church with the communications media.

1 2 3 4 5 6 7 8 9   14 13 12 11 10

Contents

Saint Ann

Saint Ann is the mother of Mary and the grandmother of Jesus.

Ann was married to a good man named Joachim. Joachim was wealthy. He had lambs and sheep that gave him wool. Joachim gave one part of his riches as an offering to those who served the Lord. He gave the

second part to the widows and the orphans. He kept only the third part for himself.

Ann and Joachim had everything they wanted—except a baby. People used to say, "God has not blessed them with a child." This made Ann and Joachim very sad.

One day, when she was quite elderly, Ann was walking in her garden. When she looked up toward the sky, she saw a nest of sparrows in a tree. Ann started to cry. Then she prayed, "O Lord, I am not like the birds of the sky. Even they have their little birds.

"I am not like the other animals either, because all animals on earth have the young ones you give them.

"O Lord, I am not like this water, because even it is filled with living creatures."

Then suddenly an angel of the Lord appeared to Ann. The angel said, "God has heard your prayer, Ann. You will have a baby. Your child will be very important for the salvation of the world."

Ann was so happy that she made a special promise to God. She said, "If I bring a baby into the world, I will give my child as an offering to the Lord my God. My girl or boy will become God's servant."

Time passed. Then, just as the angel had said, the special day arrived. Ann had a beautiful baby girl! Ann and Joachim named her Mary.

When Mary was still very young, Ann and Joachim brought her to live in God's temple. They did this to fulfill the promise that Ann had made to the angel.

History books do not tell us about the life of Saint Ann. All that we know about her comes from stories the early Christians wrote down. The Christians told these stories to their children. These children grew up and told the stories to their own children. This happened for hundreds and hundreds of years. The stories about Saint Ann spread through the eastern part of the world first, then through the western part.

Around the year 550, the Roman Emperor Justinian built the first church in honor of Saint Ann. It was in a large city called Constantinople. One thousand years later, Pope Gregory XIII set aside a special day to be Saint Ann's feast day.

Many artists have drawn or painted pictures of Ann with baby Mary in her arms or by her side. They have also shown Saint Ann with Joachim presenting young

Mary in the temple or teaching little Mary to read. Some artists have even drawn Saint Ann with the grown-up Mary and baby Jesus, showing the grandmother, mother, and child.

Saint Ann is the patron saint of mothers of families and of women who desire to have a child. Ann is also the patron of weavers, tailors, and manufacturers of brooms because she taught Mary how to weave, sew, and clean the house. Ann's name means "grace" or "God's favored one."

Many churches all over the world are dedicated to Saint Ann. A famous and beautiful one is in Quebec, Canada. People from all over the world go there to honor Saint Ann. They ask her to pray to God for them. July 26 is the feast of both Saint Ann and Saint Joachim.

Saint Joseph

We call Saint Joseph the legal father of Jesus. Even though God was Jesus' real Father, Joseph is the man who took care of baby Jesus and helped him to grow up. The Gospels of Luke and Matthew tell us about Joseph. He was a descendent of King David. We also find some legends about Joseph in the writings of

the early Christians. Here is one of them—the legend of the walking stick.

One day, there was a commotion in the village of Nazareth. Some men came with a special message. "All the unmarried men should present themselves before the high priest," they cried out. "And each one should bring his own walking stick."

The time had arrived to find a husband for Mary. It was believed that if something special happened to one of the walking sticks, it would be a sign that its owner was chosen by God to become Mary's husband.

Joseph was working in his carpenter's shop. As soon as he heard the call of the town messengers, he stopped and listened. He went with the other men to see the high priest. The high priest collected all the walking sticks the men had brought. Then he entered into the sanctuary to pray. After praying, he gave back all the walking sticks to the men. Nothing special had happened. But when the priest was about to hand back Joseph's stick, a dove landed on it.

This was the long-awaited sign! God wanted Joseph to be Mary's husband!

Whether or not this legend is true, Joseph really did become engaged to marry Mary. They lived in Nazareth, a little town in Galilee. When Joseph found out that Mary was expecting a baby before their wedding, he felt upset. He decided to end their engagement without saying a word to anyone.

Then, one night, an angel of the Lord appeared to him. The angel said, "Joseph, do not be afraid to marry Mary. The baby that will be born to her is the work of the Holy Spirit. You will call him Jesus, which means, 'God saves.' He will save his people from their sins."

Joseph, who was an obedient and good man, believed the angel. He accepted his mission to be the husband of Mary.

At that time, Emperor Augustus ordered all the people of the Roman Empire to be counted in a census. Every man had to return to the city from which his family had come. Joseph had to travel to Bethlehem, the city of King David. He brought Mary with him. During this trip, the time arrived for Mary to have her baby. There was no room for Mary and Joseph in the inns of Bethlehem. So Joseph found a cave that was used as

a stable for animals. Jesus was born there. Mary wrapped him in swaddling clothes to keep him warm. Then she placed him in a manger to sleep.

Once again, an angel came to Joseph in a dream. "King Herod is searching for the child," the angel said. "He wants to kill him. You must take Jesus and Mary and run away to Egypt!" Again, Joseph obeyed. He took Mary and baby Jesus and started out on a long journey. He only returned to Nazareth when the angel of the Lord told him that those who wanted to hurt Jesus were dead.

We meet Joseph for the last time in the Gospel of Luke. It's the scene in which he and Mary are searching for Jesus at the Temple in Jerusalem. Jesus is twelve, and his parents have just realized that he is missing. Why isn't he traveling home with the rest of his relatives?

Mary and Joseph finally find him in the Temple. He is listening to the teachers and asking them questions.

Joseph probably died before Jesus began his public life. In fact, after the Temple episode, the Gospels no longer mention Joseph. He is not there standing under the cross with Mary as Jesus is dying. But we do find other stories about Saint Joseph in the writings of some of the early Christians. They tell us that Joseph probably worked with wood. Today we would call him a carpenter.

Artists have painted many pictures of Saint Joseph with Mary at the birth of Jesus in Bethlehem. Another popular painting of Saint Joseph shows him leading the donkey carrying Mary and Jesus when the Holy Family ran away to Egypt.

Because Saint Joseph could only find a cave for himself and Mary to stay in at Bethlehem, he is the protector of the poor and the underprivileged. Saint Joseph is the patron of carpenters, too. We also pray to Saint Joseph to protect those who are dying. He must have had a very beautiful death, because Jesus and

Mary were there to help him. Pope Pius IX named Saint Joseph the Patron of the Universal Church—God's family—in 1870. Many churches all over the world are dedicated to him. One of the most famous ones is Saint Joseph's Oratory in Montreal, Canada.

The name Joseph means "enhanced by God." Joseph has two feast days. On March 19, we celebrate the feast of Saint Joseph, the Husband of Mary. On May 1, we celebrate the feast of Saint Joseph the Worker.

Saint John the Baptist

Saint Luke's Gospel tells us about the parents and the early life of Saint John the Baptist. It says that at the time of Herod, king of Judea, there was a priest named Zechariah. His wife was named Elizabeth. She was a descendent of Aaron.

Elizabeth and Zechariah were holy people. But they didn't have any children, because Elizabeth could not have a baby. Even though they wanted a child, the couple was already too elderly.

One day, while Zechariah was carrying out a celebration before the Lord, an angel appeared to him. "Soon you will have a son," the angel told him.

"But how can this be?" Zechariah asked. "My wife and I are too old."

"I am Gabriel," the angel answered. "I have been sent by God to bring you this good news. But because you did not believe me, you will not be able to speak until the baby is born."

In the meantime, the angel Gabriel had also appeared to Mary to announce to her the birth of Jesus. Gabriel told Mary that Elizabeth, her cousin, was expecting a baby boy. Not long after, Mary went to visit Elizabeth. She entered her house and greeted her. As soon as Elizabeth heard Mary's voice, she exclaimed, "Blessed are you among women and blessed is the fruit of your womb. When I heard your greeting, the baby leapt for joy in my womb."

This was the first meeting between the cousins John and Jesus.

Eight days after John was born, Zechariah and Elizabeth brought him to the Temple for a special celebration. All the relatives wanted to name him Zechariah, after his father. But Elizabeth said, "No, he will be called John."

"No one in your family has this name!" the relatives cried. Then they made signs to Zechariah to ask him what name he wanted to give the baby. Zechariah gestured for a writing tablet. He wrote, "His name is John." Suddenly, Zechariah was able to speak again. He began to praise God!

Everyone who had seen what had happened was astonished. "Who will this child be?" they asked. They knew that John was someone special.

All the Gospel writers agree that John the Baptist is the one that Isaiah the prophet was talking about when he wrote, "A voice cries out in the desert, 'Prepare the way of the Lord.'" John's mission was to announce to everyone that Jesus was coming.

When John grew up, he lived in the desert. He wore clothes made from the hide of a camel, with a piece of leather for a belt. He ate locusts and wild honey.

While John was in the desert praying and doing penance, people from all over Judea and the city of Jerusalem came to him to be baptized. One day, even Jesus, John's cousin, came. John didn't want to baptize Jesus at first. John told Jesus, "I'm the one who needs to be baptized by *you*!" But John gave in because this is what Jesus wanted.

At the moment John baptized Jesus, the heavens opened and God the Father said, "This is my beloved Son in whom I am well pleased."

John always taught the truth. This got him into trouble with some people, including King Herod. The king had married Herodias, the wife of his brother Philip. This was the wrong thing to do. John kept telling the king that it was wrong. So the king finally put him in prison. Herodias was upset with John. Having him in prison wasn't enough for her. She wanted to get rid of him.

One day, Salome, the daughter of Herodias, performed a dance during a banquet that King Herod gave. She was so good at it and so beautiful that Herod promised to give her anything she wanted. Salome, getting the idea from her mother, asked King Herod for the head of John the Baptist. The king didn't want to kill John. But he had to keep his promise in front of all his guests. So the king had John's head cut off.

Saint John the Baptist is so important that he is the only saint who has one feast day to celebrate his birth—June 24—and another to remember his death—August 29. Saint John the Baptist is the protector of orphans.

This is because, long ago, babies without parents were left near the baptismal font in Catholic churches so they could be cared for by the Church. Saint John the Baptist is also the patron of religious groups that help persons who have been condemned to death.

The name John means, "God is merciful," or "gift of the Lord."

Saint Peter

One day, a large crowd came to listen to Jesus on the shore of Lake Gennesaret. Some fishermen were also there washing their nets. Jesus climbed into the boat that belonged to a fisherman named Simon. Jesus asked Simon to row away from the shore. He wanted to continue to teach the people from the boat.

When Jesus had finished speaking, he turned to Simon. "Row out into deeper water," he said, "and lower your nets to catch some fish." Simon answered, "Master, we have worked hard all night and have caught nothing. But if you say so, I'll lower the nets again." Soon Simon and his friends caught so many fish that their nets started to tear and their boat was ready to sink!

Simon and the other fishermen were amazed. Then Jesus told them, "Do not be afraid. Follow me. From now on you will catch men instead of fish." Then Simon and the other fishermen left everything behind and followed Jesus.

Simon was an honest and simple man. He put his whole heart into everything he did. Jesus chose Simon to be one of the twelve apostles, his closest followers. The other apostles were Andrew, Simon's brother; James and John, the sons of Zebedee; Philip; Bartholomew; Thomas; Matthew; James, son of Alphaeus; Simon; Judas, son of James; and Judas Iscariot, who betrayed Jesus.

Simon was the first apostle to believe that Jesus is the Son of God. Jesus changed Simon's name to Peter.

Jesus told him, "You are Peter, and on this rock I will build my Church. To you I will give the keys to the Kingdom of Heaven." Jesus chose Peter to be the first pope of the Catholic Church.

Like the other apostles, Peter listened to the parables that Jesus taught. He saw the many miracles that Jesus worked for different people. Sometimes Peter was brave. Sometimes he was afraid. Sometimes he did or said things without thinking

One time, Jesus came walking on the stormy sea toward his apostles. The apostles were very frightened in their boat. They thought Jesus was a ghost! Peter called out, "Jesus, if it's really you, tell me to come to you walking on the water." Jesus said to him, "Come!" Peter got out of the boat and began to walk on the water. But the wind frightened him, and he began to sink.

"Lord, save me!" he cried. Jesus immediately reached out his hand and caught Peter. Then Jesus gently scolded him, saying, "Man of little faith, why did you doubt?"

Another time, after the Last Supper, Jesus went with his apostles toward the Mount of Olives. As they were walking, Jesus said, "Tonight you will all fall away."

Peter shouted back loudly, "Even if everyone else disowns you, I will never disown you!" Jesus looked sadly at Peter. He replied, "Before the rooster crows you will deny me three times, Peter."

Then Jesus went to pray in a place called Gethsemane. Meanwhile, the apostles were so tired they fell asleep. But the soldiers were already coming to arrest Jesus. Peter woke up and wanted to defend Jesus. He swung his sword and cut the ear of the high priest's servant. Jesus had to tell him to put his sword away.

That night, Peter lied three times. He was afraid to get into trouble, so he said he didn't know Jesus. When the rooster crowed at dawn, Peter remembered what Jesus had said. He was very sorry for having denied Jesus, and he began to cry.

After the death and resurrection of Jesus, Peter became a strong man. He gathered the apostles together. When the Holy Spirit came down upon them, they became missionaries and traveled all over the world to preach and teach about Jesus.

During the persecution of Emperor Nero, Saint Peter was put into prison. He died as a martyr in Rome, probably around the year 67. He was crucified upside down, because he said he wasn't worthy to die exactly as Jesus had.

Many paintings show Saint Peter with Jesus. Some show Peter holding the keys of the kingdom of heaven. Other symbols that remind us of Peter are the fisherman's boat, the rooster that stands for the times Peter betrayed Jesus, and the cross, a sign of his martyrdom.

In the Basilica of Saint Peter in the Vatican, where Peter is buried, there is a large bronze statue showing him in the act of blessing. It's a custom that each visitor touches the foot of the statue with his or her right hand before making the sign of the cross. This gesture has been repeated so many times that the statue's foot has been worn smooth.

Saint Peter is the protector of fishermen, net makers, and builders of bridges and ships.

The feast of Saints Peter and Paul is one of the most important saints' days. We celebrate it on June 29.

Saint Paul

Even though Saint Paul didn't know Jesus in person, many people call him "the thirteenth apostle." This is because Paul preached and wrote so well about Jesus.

Paul was born after Jesus' death, between the years 5 and 10, in Tarsus, a busy city in Cilicia. His father had a successful business selling tents. The people who lived in Tarsus had a right to Roman citizenship. According to the custom of those days, they received two names—a Hebrew name and a Latin name. Paul's Hebrew name was Saul, which means, "requested by God." His Latin name, Paulus or Paul, means "little one." People may have called him this because he wasn't very tall.

Saul spoke two languages, Hebrew and Greek. His mother and father taught him Hebrew. He learned Greek at school. When he was a young man, Saul traveled to Jerusalem to study his Jewish religion with Gamaliel, the best Jewish teacher at that time.

In Jerusalem, Saul became an enemy of the Christians. He thought that the followers of Jesus were spreading false teachings about God. Saul believed that he was doing the right thing when he got permission to arrest Christians and throw them into jail.

But one day, when Saul was on his way to the city of Damascus to arrest more Christians, he saw a light from heaven. It was brighter than the sun! Saul fell to the ground. He heard a voice say, "Saul, Saul, why are you persecuting me?"

Saul was very surprised. "Who are you, Lord?" he asked.

The voice answered, "I am Jesus, the one you are persecuting. Now get up and go into the city, and you will be told what you must do."

The men who were with Saul were astonished. They had heard the voice, but they hadn't seen anyone.

Saul got up from the ground, but he couldn't see. Someone took him by the hand and brought him to Damascus. For three days, Saul wouldn't eat or drink anything. He was praying and trying to understand what God wanted him to do. Then God sent a Christian named Ananias to visit Saul. When Ananias laid his hands on Saul's eyes, Saul could see again! At that moment, Saul became a new man. He became Paul, the apostle of Jesus.

Paul was baptized and stayed a few more days in Damascus. Those who heard him preach about Jesus, God's Son, were surprised. They asked, "Isn't this the

man who came here to arrest the Christians? Now he's a Christian too!"

After his conversion Paul went to the desert to pray and think about all that had happened to him. Then he went back to Damascus to preach. He also traveled to Jerusalem to meet Peter. He asked Peter to teach him more about Jesus.

Paul had persecuted the Christians. Now that he was a Christian himself, some people began to persecute him. But Paul was brave. He became a tireless traveler. He went everywhere he could to teach people about Jesus. And everywhere he went he founded churches.

After Paul visited different places and helped people become Christians, he wrote them letters. In his letters, Paul encouraged the people to be good followers of Jesus, and he taught them how. We can still read Saint Paul's letters today. They're in the section of the Bible called the New Testament. Here is part of one of Saint Paul's most famous and beautiful letters, his First Letter to the Corinthians:

If I did not love others, I would be nothing more
than a noisy gong or a clanging cymbal.
Love is kind and patient,
never jealous, boastful, proud, or rude.
Love isn't selfish or quick-tempered.
It doesn't keep a record of wrongs that others do.
Love rejoices in the truth,
but not in evil.
Love is always supportive,
loyal, hopeful, and trusting.
Love never fails!

Paul had to suffer very much for believing in Jesus and for teaching others about him. He was put in jail, whipped, and even shipwrecked. Around the year 67, during the time the Emperor Nero was persecuting the Christians of Rome, Paul was finally sentenced to death. An executioner cut off his head.

Artists often show Saint Paul as an elderly man holding a sword, the symbol of his martyrdom.

People who have trouble seeing often pray to Saint Paul, because he knew what it was like to be blind. Other persons pray to Paul for protection against storms at sea, because he was in a shipwreck. Saint Paul is also the patron saint of manufacturers of baskets and rope, because one time he had to escape from his enemies in a basket hanging from a rope. We celebrate the Conversion of Saint Paul on January 25. He also shares a feast day with Saint Peter on June 29.

Saint Cecilia

History doesn't tell us much about Cecilia's life. We do know that she was one of the saints most honored by the early Christians. We also know that she was born into a noble family. Cecilia's father was a Roman senator. Her family was quite wealthy.

After Cecilia received a visit from an angel, she promised Jesus she would dedicate her whole life to him. But her father wanted her to be married. He even arranged for her to wed a pagan nobleman named Valerian. Cecilia had to obey. On the night following their wedding, Cecilia told Valerian that she was dedicated to Jesus. She also asked him to become a Christian.

The young man, moved by her great faith, agreed to learn about Jesus and be baptized. He hoped that after he became a Christian he would see the angel who had visited Cecilia.

Valerian asked where he could find Pope Urban. He wanted the pope to baptize him. After he was baptized, Valerian returned home. The angel was waiting for him, right next to Cecilia!

The angel gave Cecilia and Valerian a crown of lilies and roses that came from heaven. Then Valerian began to wish that his brother, Tiburtius, would become a Christian, too. Soon Tiburtius was baptized. After that, Cecilia, Valerian, and Tiburtius dedicated themselves to burying the Christian martyrs who had been put to death by Almachio, one of the Roman officials. When Almachio found out that Valerian and Tiburtius were Christians, he had them killed too.

After Cecilia buried Valerian and Tiburtius, guards also came to arrest her. Before she was taken away, Cecilia was able to donate her riches to the poor and give her house to the Church.

Cecilia was condemned to death for being a Christian. The emperor had her put in a very hot room to stop her from breathing. But she didn't die. Next, he ordered a soldier to cut off her head. Still, Cecilia didn't die right away. She held out three fingers of one hand and one finger of the other hand. By doing this, Cecilia showed that she believed in the Blessed Trinity—one God in three divine Persons.

In the Middle Ages, people began to honor Saint Cecilia as the patron saint of musicians. This is probably because of a story that was written about her wedding. Part of the story said, "Cecilia sang in her heart to the Lord while the musical instruments played for her wedding."

Ever since then, many artists have shown Cecilia as a musician. She's often pictured playing an organ. At other times, she's playing a harp, or is shown with sheets of music. In some paintings, musical angels surround her. Other pictures of Saint Cecilia show her with a sword, the symbol of her martyrdom, and a crown of flowers.

Because Cecilia is the patron saint of musicians, some great musicians have composed sacred works in her honor. Many academies and schools of music are also named after her.

We celebrate the feast of Saint Cecilia every year on November 22. The name Cecilia means "the blind one."

Saint Helen the Empress

Helen was born around the year 248 in Bithynia, a part of the Roman Empire. Her family was poor. As a young woman, Helen worked in a stable. Next, she was a maid in an inn. But when she was in her twenties, she married an important official of the Roman army. His name was Constantius Chlorus. Soon Helen and Constantius had a son. They named him Constantine.

After a while, Constantius became even more important in the army. Then he was appointed ruler of the western part of the Roman Empire. Since Roman law did not recognize a marriage between a nobleman and a working-class woman, Constantius decided to end his marriage to Helen. He divorced her and married the stepdaughter of Emperor Maximian. To make things worse, he took Constantine with him when he left. Helen was heartbroken. She loved Constantius and their son Constantine very much. But there was nothing she could do.

Later on, when Constantius died, Constantine became emperor. He brought his mother, Helen, to live with him at the palace. Helen was about sixty-five years old by this time. Constantine gave her the title of empress. He even had coins made in her honor.

It was the year 306, and Helen had become a Christian. As the empress, she could finally fulfill her dream of helping others. Helen used part of the imperial treasures to help the needy. She gave clothes to the poor. She invited the hungry to eat at the palace. She freed prisoners who had been unjustly condemned. She also had many new churches built and decorated them with beautiful artwork and gold. In everything she did, Helen witnessed to her faith in Jesus and passed it on to others.

Meanwhile, Constantine, who was not a Christian, was preparing for an important battle. Not long before the battle, he saw a large cross in the sky. These words were written on the cross: "In this sign you will conquer."

Constantine didn't understand what the vision meant. That same night, he had a dream. Jesus appeared to him holding a cross. Jesus told Constantine, "Place an image of the cross on the shields of your soldiers and on the flag you carry in battle." Constantine obeyed, and he and his army won the battle. After this happened, Constantine sent his mother Helen to Jerusalem. He wanted her to search for the wooden cross on which Jesus had been crucified. The cross had been kept by the early Christians. But it had been lost later when the Romans scattered the Christians and Jews.

At Calvary and at the Holy Sepulcher (where Jesus was buried before he rose from the dead) another

emperor had built two pagan temples. He had done this on purpose to try to destroy the memory of Jesus. Emperor Constantine ordered the pagan temples to be knocked down. Then he had a large Christian church built in their place.

Helen was already old by this time, but she wanted to make sure that the work on the church was well done. She visited the places where Jesus had lived and died. She prayed at the tomb in which the body of Jesus had been laid. On Mount Calvary, Helen watched the men who were digging to build the new church. They heard her say, "I am an empress on a throne, and the cross of my Lord is buried in the dust! I am surrounded by gold, and the triumph of Christ is in ruins!"

Helen then ordered the workers to dig up a certain area of the hill. There she found three crosses. Helen knew that one of the three crosses was the one Jesus had died on. The other two belonged to the two criminals who had been crucified with Jesus. But how could she tell which cross was which?

Helen went to a holy bishop named Macarius. He had an idea. "We will bring the three crosses to a sick person. We will pray and have the sick person touch each of the crosses." This is what they did. As soon as the woman who was sick touched the cross of Jesus, she was cured!

When the workers were digging on Mount Calvary, Helen also found a wooden sign with writing in Hebrew, Latin, and Greek. It was the sign that had been placed at the top of the cross of Jesus. It said, "Jesus of Nazareth, King of the Jews." The workmen also dug up some nails. Helen believed that they were from the cross of Jesus. She brought the nails, the sign, and some small pieces of the cross of Jesus back to Rome with her. She also brought some thorns from Jesus' crown of thorns, and a large quantity of the soil on which Jesus had walked during his passion. Helen kept these precious relics in her palace in Rome. Later, Constantine had the palace turned into a church. Today this beautiful church is called the Basilica of the Holy Cross of Jerusalem.

Before he died, Emperor Constantine was also baptized a Christian. He allowed all Christians to practice their religion without being persecuted.

Because she found the true cross of Jesus, Saint Helen is invoked by those who search for lost objects. She is also the patron of those who make nails and needles.

Helen's name means "splendor of the sun," or "luminous one." We celebrate her feast day on August 18.

Saint Lucy

Lucy was born in Syracuse, on the island of Sicily in Italy. Her father died when she was about six years old. Lucy and her mother were Christians. Following the custom of those days, her mother chose a young man for Lucy to marry. But there was a problem. Lucy had secretly promised to give up marriage so that she could dedicate herself to Jesus.

Lucy traveled with her mother, Eutychia, to the city of Catania. They went to pray at the tomb of Saint Agatha. Eutychia was very sick. Lucy wanted Saint Agatha to ask God to cure her. At Saint Agatha's shrine, Lucy made a promise to give everything she had to the poor.

At the shrine, Saint Agatha appeared to Lucy and her mother. She promised that Lucy's mother would get well. She also told Lucy that she would soon die as a martyr.

When they returned home, Eutychia did get better. Lucy gave away all her things to the poor. She also told her mother that she couldn't get married because she had dedicated herself to Jesus. Her mother was grateful that she had been cured, so she allowed Lucy to end her engagement. But the bridegroom-to-be was infuriated! He was a pagan, and he went to one of the city officials and reported that Lucy was a Christian. Because it was against the law to be a Christian, the official had Lucy thrown in jail. The guards tried over and over again to make Lucy deny her faith in Jesus. They threatened to lock her up in a sinful place. But when the soldiers tried to move her, she became so heavy that she wouldn't budge. Next, they poured boiling tar and oil over her, and put her on burning coals. But God protected her, and she wasn't hurt. Finally, they killed Lucy by cutting her throat with a sword. It was the year 304.

Saint Lucy makes us think of light, which is what her name means. Tradition tells us that during her martyrdom, she was blinded. But Jesus worked a miracle and gave her back her sight. In the Scandinavian countries, Saint Lucy is honored as the one who carries light.

Families in Sweden have a special way to celebrate Saint Lucy's feast day. On that day, the youngest girl in the family gets up before dawn and dresses in a long white robe with a red belt. She wears a crown of leaves and seven candles. Then she goes from room to room to wake up the family and offer them coffee and pastries. If she has sisters, they decorate their hair with sparkles to symbolize the stars, and go with her. The boys of the family wear large straw hats and carry long sticks

decorated with little stars. On this day, Swedish families sing their version of the famous Italian song "Santa Lucia."

In some northern regions of Italy, Saint Lucy is like Santa Claus, bringing gifts to little children. On the day before her feast day, the children write her letters asking for the gifts they would like. That evening, they go to bed early so Saint Lucy won't see them. Later, Saint Lucy secretly arrives from heaven with her donkey pulling a cart full of gifts. As a sign of gratitude, it's a

custom to leave some fruit and a little milk or wine for Saint Lucy at the door of the house. Families also leave a bit of hay for her donkey.

The body of Saint Lucy is buried in the Church of Saints Jeremiah and Lucy in Venice, Italy. Saint Lucy is the patron saint of Venice, along with Saint Mark.

Many paintings show Lucy as a beautiful young girl. Sometimes she holds a plate with two eyes. This shows that she was made blind when she was tortured for being a Christian. Other symbols we sometimes find in paintings of Lucy are the palm, a lamp, a candle, and fire.

Saint Lucy is the protector of eye doctors, the blind, servants, tailors, and weavers. She is prayed to for the cure of sicknesses of the eyes and throat.

Saint Lucy's feast day is celebrated on December 13.

Saint Ambrose

Ambrose's mother and father were Christians. They lived in Trier, an important Roman city on the border of Germany. That is where Ambrose was born around the year 339.

The Roman emperor made Ambrose's father the governor of Gaul. His mother also belonged to a noble

family. Ambrose's parents hoped that he would grow up and become a politician like his father. They sent him to study Greek, Latin, and the law. Ambrose also became very good at making speeches.

When he was thirty years old, Ambrose became a governor. He went to live in the big city of Milan. Some years later, the bishop of Milan died. Everyone was having a hard time deciding on a new bishop.

All the people knew and respected Ambrose. But no one had thought of electing him as bishop. He wasn't even a priest. The story goes that a little boy cried out in church, "Ambrose, bishop!" The people who heard him said, "This must be a sign of God's will!" Then everyone wanted Ambrose to become the new bishop.

At first, Ambrose didn't want to accept this responsibility. But the people kept insisting. So, in just a few days, Ambrose was ordained a priest and then a bishop. He gave away all that he had to the poor. From that time on, Ambrose wholeheartedly dedicated himself to his new duties. He knew that the Bible is God's word and is very important. He began to study the Bible in a special way. He wanted to help people to understand it better. The door of Bishop Ambrose's house was always open. He never refused to listen to anyone who needed help or had a problem.

Ambrose made sure that men who were preparing to become priests were taught all they needed to know. He also began the custom of singing hymns in church. This is something that Christians in the eastern part of the world were already doing.

Bishop Ambrose was a great preacher. He invited the powerful and rich people to work for the good of everyone. He reminded them to care for the poor. Bishop Ambrose used to say to the rich, "You decorate the walls of your palaces and leave people without clothes to wear."

Ambrose's knowledge of law and his experience as a governor helped him to get along well with the leaders of the city. He defended the values of Christianity, which by then had become the main religion of the Roman Empire. Bishop Ambrose was also against any laws that would bring back the worship of pagan gods. He was never afraid to do the right thing. One time, he

even made Emperor Theodosius do a penance in front of everyone before allowing him to go into church. Ambrose did this because the emperor had unjustly killed 7,000 people during a riot.

On Easter Sunday in 387, Bishop Ambrose baptized a young man who had come from Africa to teach in Milan. This young man, who became a Christian because of the preaching and teaching of Ambrose, was named Augustine. Later on, he also became a great saint.

There is an ancient legend about Saint Ambrose. It says that one day, while Ambrose was walking in the courtyard of the church, the devil appeared to him. The devil kept trying to make Ambrose give up being a bishop. Finally, Ambrose got tired of being tempted. He lost his patience and kicked the devil! The devil flew into a column in the courtyard. He was stuck there the whole day hanging by his horns. When he managed to escape, he left two holes in the column. To this day, the people of Milan call this post "the column of the devil."

Saint Ambrose is one of the great fathers of the Church. He is also the patron of Milan. Many paintings

show Ambrose wearing the vestments of a bishop. In other paintings, there are bees near Saint Ambrose. This is because when he was a baby, a swarm of bees flew around him but didn't hurt him.

Saint Ambrose is the protector of candle makers and of beekeepers. His feast is celebrated on December 7, the date on which he was elected bishop. His name means "immortal" or "destined for eternal life."

Saint Augustine

Saint Augustine of Hippo was born in the year 354 in the city of Tagaste in Africa. His father, Patricius, was a small landowner. He wasn't a Christian. Augustine's mother was named Monica. She was a Christian, and she raised Augustine according to the teachings of the Catholic faith. Augustine was a very intelligent young man. He soon learned Latin and Greek.

When he was about seventeen years old, Augustine's parents sent him to the city of Carthage to complete his studies. When Augustine got there, he forgot all that his mother had taught him. He got mixed up with friends who cheated in school and drank. Soon Augustine began to act like his friends. Next he became a follower of a religious group called the Manichaeans. Augustine's mother tried to tell him that these people didn't believe in the one true God. But Augustine wouldn't listen. All Monica could do was pray for her son.

In the meantime, Augustine became a teacher. At first he taught in Tagaste and Carthage. When he was twenty-nine, he moved to Rome. From Rome, Augustine went to Milan. There he met Bishop Ambrose, who was a great preacher. Augustine liked to go and listen to Ambrose. There was something special about the bishop's words. They seemed to go straight to his heart and make him feel more alive.

Even though Augustine loved to learn about Jesus, he still wasn't ready to become a Christian. One day, Augustine was walking in his garden. He felt confused. He wanted to accept the Catholic faith. But he didn't want to give up the sinful things he was doing. Augustine began to pray, "Please help me, God!" Suddenly, he heard the voice of a little child singing, "Take and read. Take and read."

Augustine picked up a book of Saint Paul's letters, which had been left nearby. He opened it. The first sentence he saw was, "Put on the Lord Jesus Christ, and do not follow the flesh or its desires." This seemed like a message straight from God. Augustine decided right then to give up the sinful things he was doing. He decided to become a Christian.

While Augustine prepared for Baptism, his mother, Monica, came to Milan to be with him. She prayed with him and was very happy for him. She had prayed for many, many years that he would become a Christian. Bishop Ambrose baptized Augustine on Easter Sunday in 387. Monica died not long after. Augustine then returned to Africa. He went to Carthage and began a small community, where he lived as a monk. Next, he was ordained a priest. A few years later, the bishop of Hippo died. Augustine became the new bishop.

When some groups of people were spreading false ideas, Saint Augustine taught the truth about God. He wrote many letters and books, and he preached many sermons to help people learn to love Jesus. Two of his most famous books are *The Confessions* and *The City of God*.

Augustine lived in Hippo until he died in 430, while an army was attacking the city. His body is now kept in Pavia, Italy, in the Church of Saint Peter in the Golden Sky.

There is a beautiful legend told about Saint Augustine. The story says that one day Augustine was walking along the seashore. He was thinking very hard, trying to understand the mystery of the Holy Trinity—the mystery that teaches us that there are three Divine Persons in one God. Just then, he saw a little boy digging a hole in the sand with a small shovel. Next, the boy carried his pail to the sea and filled it with water. Then he ran and emptied the water into the hole. He filled his bucket and emptied it over and over again. Finally, Augustine asked him, "What are you doing?"

"I'm pouring all the water of the sea into this hole," the boy answered.

Augustine just smiled. But the little boy, who was really an angel, told him, "It's easier for this hole to contain all the waters of the sea than it is for your mind to contain the great mystery of the Holy Trinity." Then he disappeared.

In many paintings, Saint Augustine is shown with a monk's habit and a leather belt, or wearing the vestments of a bishop. Some paintings also show the child with the shovel. This reminds us of the legend about the mystery of the Holy Trinity.

Saint Augustine is the patron of theologians and of booksellers. His feast falls on August 28, the day after the feast day of his mother, Saint Monica.

The name Augustine means "the revered one" and "consecrated herald."

Saint Benedict

Benedict was born in Norcia, Italy, around the year 480. He belonged to a noble and wealthy family. When he was a young man, he was sent to Rome to study, as all the sons of well-to-do families did. But there was a lot of evil and violence in Rome at that time. Benedict became so disgusted with life in this big city that he decided to leave everything behind and

consecrate himself to God. He was following the example of his sister, Scholastica. She had already decided to consecrate herself to God.

At the age of seventeen, Benedict left Rome. He stopped first at the Italian village of Enfide. There he began to live like a monk. Next, he continued on his journey and arrived in Subiaco.

In Subiaco, Benedict met a monk named Romano, who lived in a nearby monastery. Romano gave Benedict a monk's habit. He also showed Benedict a cave in the mountains where he could live alone, meditate, and pray. Every day Romano brought Benedict bread and water to eat. Benedict spent three years in the cave as a hermit. Then, a community of monks asked him to become the abbot of their monastery.

Benedict agreed. But one of the monks thought he was too strict and tried to poison him! Benedict left there and returned to Subiaco, where he began to preach. He was becoming famous as a holy person, and many people were coming to see him. Some men wanted to stay and serve the Lord with him, so Benedict founded his first monastery.

As more monks joined him, Benedict opened more monasteries. Each monastery was made up of twelve monks who obeyed their own superior. The rule that Benedict gave his monks to follow was very wise and practical. It taught them how to serve the Lord in every situation. The Benedictine Rule said, "If you want to serve God, *ora et labora*." That means, "pray and work." Until the time of Benedict, many people thought of work as something slaves did, or as a punishment from God. Benedict, instead, taught that work is something good and important.

Benedict's monks spent the twenty-four hours of each day alternating hours of work with hours of prayer. Some times of prayer were during the day. Others were during the night. The rule gave instructions for everything, including the meals the monks ate and the way they cared for their fields and gardens. The rule even explained what the monks should study. Every monk prayed and worked, contributing to the needs of the monastery. There was no time for laziness!

Even though Benedict wanted all the monks to follow the rule that he gave them, he knew that rules should

be applied with love to each individual person. He treated the elderly and sick monks with special kindness. Things were not as strict for them as they were for the others. He even made sure that those who did more tiring work were given a bit more to eat.

One day Totila, king of the Goths, wanted to find out if Benedict was as holy as everyone said he was. He made an appointment to see Benedict. But instead of going himself, he sent his attendant Rigo. Totila had Rigo dress like a king in order to fool Benedict. But as soon as he saw Rigo, Benedict said, "My son, take off immediately the garment that covers you, because it does not belong to you."

Rigo rushed back to King Totila and told him what had happened. When Totila finally came in person, Benedict scolded him for his cruelty and invited him to change his life. Benedict predicted that Totila would reign for nine years and then die. And that's just what happened.

Benedict died in 547. A story says that he died a few days after he had his tomb prepared. He was surrounded by his monks, and his arms were raised to heaven.

In paintings, Saint Benedict is shown wearing a black habit with a hood and a large cape. Two of his symbols are a book, which represents the rule he wrote for monks, and the crow that saved him by snatching the bread that the envious monk Fiorenzo tried to poison him with. Benedict's name means "he who wishes well." Saint Benedict is the patron of Europe. We celebrate his feast on July 11.

Saint Francis

Francis was the son of Peter Bernardone, a rich merchant who sold expensive fabrics. Francis was born in 1181 in Assisi, Italy. A legend says that he was born like Jesus—in a stable, between an ox and a donkey.

Francis was intelligent and lively. In school, he learned grammar, French, and Latin. But what he liked best was reading French stories about the heroic deeds of King Arthur and the Knights of the Round Table.

Francis was kind even when others insulted him. He had the reputation of being very generous, both with the poor and with his friends. He loved parties. He would organize them and pay all the expenses, too. Francis also had a beautiful voice. He liked to wander the streets singing and making people happy.

When he was twenty years old, Francis joined in a battle against the neighboring town of Perugia. He was captured by the enemy. When he was finally set free, Francis went home. But his time in prison had changed him. Now he felt a great emptiness in his heart. He no longer wanted to spend all his time at parties.

A nobleman from Assisi was preparing to fight to defend some property of the Church. Francis had always wanted to become a knight. He decided to go with the nobleman. *If I fight with honor,* he thought, *I might finally become a knight.*

Francis set out on this new adventure. But the journey lasted only one day. That night, in the town of Spoleto, he heard a voice say to him, "Francis, is it better to serve the master or the servant?" "The master, of course," Francis answered. "Return to your city and you will be told what to do," the voice replied.

The next morning, Francis returned to Assisi. He tried going to parties again, but things just weren't the same. Soon he began begging for food and money for the poor. He hugged people with leprosy. He spent more time praying. One day, while he was praying in the little church of Saint Damien, Francis heard Jesus say to him from the crucifix, "Francis, repair my house, because it is collapsing." Francis finally knew what he was supposed to do! He went to his father's shop, took a roll of very expensive fabric, and sold it. Then he brought the money to the priest at Saint Damien's and offered to help repair the church.

The priest refused the money. He was afraid that Peter Bernardone would be angry because of what Francis had done. He was right! Francis's father was very upset when he found out. He even went to the

bishop demanding that he tell Francis to give back the money. A meeting between Francis and his father was held in the public square in front of the bishop. The bishop asked Francis to give back the money to his father. Then Francis surprised everyone. He said that from that moment on, his only father would be his Father in heaven. While he was saying this, he took off all his clothes and gave them back to his father. Peter Bernadone was so ashamed of Francis that he rushed home. But the bishop opened his arms and covered Francis with his own cloak.

Francis had taken a big step in leaving his family and money behind. For a whole year, he wandered through the fields, forests, and hills. He prayed and meditated in caves. Then he returned to Assisi to help the lepers and to repair the walls of the Church of Saint Damien. He went from street to street shouting, "He who gives me a stone will be rewarded. He who gives me two stones will be doubly rewarded!"

People wondered, "Isn't this poor beggar Francis Bernadone, who used to be the life of every party? What's happened to him?" Some people made fun of him. Others felt sorry for him. His own father was still ashamed of him.

After Saint Damien's, Francis repaired other churches. Assisi had many of them. One morning, Francis listened as a priest explained the words of the Gospel. Father said, "Jesus told his disciples that they must not keep gold or money, or carry a saddlebag or purse. They should go without a walking stick and shoes. They should not have two robes, only one. They should only preach the Kingdom of God and penance."

After he heard this, Francis gave up his shoes and walking stick. He chose to live in absolute poverty, just like Jesus.

Soon others also gave up their comfortable lives and came to join Francis. This was the start of the Franciscan Order. In the beginning, there were twelve in the group—just like the first apostles. They prayed and helped the poor and the sick. More and more young men continued to join them. Later on, some young women of Assisi's noble and wealthy families also wanted to live as Francis and his companions did. Clare Offreduccio was the first to come. She cut her long, lovely hair, dressed in

a poor habit, and wore wooden sandals. Like Francis
and his brothers, she made the vows of poverty, chastity,
and obedience.

Here's one of the favorite stories told about Saint
Francis: In 1223, Francis was visiting the town of Greccio
just a few days before Christmas. He wanted to show
the townspeople how Jesus had been born in a poor
stable. He asked a good man named John to go into
the forest and prepare a real manger with hay and to
bring an ox and a donkey. Families came from nearby
farmhouses, brightening the night with the torches they

carried. The forest echoed with voices and songs as Mass was celebrated beside the manger. It was the first Christmas crèche.

Francis died in October 1226 at the age of forty-five. He asked to be brought to the little chapel where he had begun his religious life. There, as he wished, he was laid on the ground. Francis sang praises to the Lord even as he was dying.

One of the most famous things Francis wrote is *The Canticle of the Creatures*. He dictated it to Brother Leo so it could be put to music for people to sing in praise of God. It's believed to be the oldest and most precious poem written in the Italian language. Saint Francis is the patron of Italy and of many cities all over the world. San Francisco in California is named after him! We celebrate the feast day of Saint Francis on October 4.

Saint Anthony of Padua

Fernando, the future Saint Anthony, was born in Lisbon, Portugal, in 1195. His father, Martin, was a noble knight of King Alfonse.

Fernando was a good student. He lived a happy-go-lucky life and had all that he wanted. When he was

fifteen, he surprised everyone by announcing that he was going to enter the Augustinian monastery in Lisbon. He wanted to become a monk.

Years later, Fernando, now Father Fernando, was living at a monastery in the city of Coimbra. One day, five Franciscan friars arrived in Coimbra. They were poorly dressed and had only bread and water to eat. They stopped at Fernando's monastery to spend the night. The friars were on their way to Morocco to preach the Gospel, which was against the law there. Once they arrived in Africa, all five of them were imprisoned and killed.

The courage of these friars impressed Fernando so deeply that he decided to follow the friars' example and become a follower of Saint Francis. After obtaining permission from his superior, he left the Augustinians and entered the Franciscan Order. As a sign of the new life he was beginning, Fernando took a new name— Anthony. He put on the rough robe of the Franciscans. Soon he was on his way to Morocco to preach and teach about Jesus. But on the voyage, he came down with malaria. He was so sick that his superiors told him to return to Portugal. During the trip back, Anthony's ship ran into a terrible storm. The ship went aground on the coast of Sicily in Italy. Some kind fishermen brought Father Anthony to a nearby Franciscan monastery.

Not long after, Saint Francis, who was still alive at that time, called all his friars to meet in Assisi. Anthony started off on the journey. Over 3,000 friars had come to Assisi. They were discussing important things like the new rule and the invitation for missionaries to go to Germany and other countries.

Anthony hoped that someone would choose him to be part of a mission. But no one did. The other friars didn't know him. Everyone thought he was young and not much use for anything.

When the meeting ended, Anthony asked a friar named Gratian if he could go home with him. Friar Gratian said yes. So Anthony spent a year with the friars of Montepaolo doing whatever humble chores needed to be done. In the meantime, he meditated and prayed.

One day, the friars of Montepaolo went to the town of Forli, where some young men were being ordained

as priests. The priest who was supposed to preach never came. None of the other priests had prepared a homily. And no one wanted to volunteer to preach. Finally, Anthony was asked to speak. At first, he hesitated. But he had made a vow of obedience, and he knew he had to obey. When Anthony began to speak, everyone was amazed. His words were so clear, and holy, and wise. *Where did he get all this?* the other friars wondered. *All he's been doing is washing dishes and floors!*

News of Anthony's wonderful talent soon reached his superiors in Assisi. They immediately assigned Anthony to preach in the villages and in castles. He became a traveling preacher bringing the Word of God throughout all of Italy and France.

Anthony spoke to the crowds in their local languages. When he was preaching to scholarly men, he spoke in Latin. He showed mercy with the poor. But he was strict with the powerful and severe with unjust moneylenders and the enemies of the Church. People used to call him "the hammer of the heretics" because he sternly corrected all those who were teaching false ideas about God and the Catholic Church. His preaching touched people's hearts. They never got tired of listening to him.

Later on, Anthony was put in charge of the Franciscans living in northern Italy. He was always on the move. He visited monasteries and founded new ones. He encouraged vocations, preached, and converted many people.

Finally, toward the end of his life, when he was tired and sick, Anthony settled in the city of Padua. It was almost Lent. Anthony probably knew that he didn't have long to live. He decided to prepare for Easter by preaching every day. No one had ever done this before. The crowds that came to listen to Anthony grew larger every day. The church wasn't large enough to hold all the people, so Anthony took them to the fields outside the city. Many people wanted to touch him. Some women even carried scissors to cut off a piece of his habit!

Anthony's words really changed hearts and minds. People stopped quarreling. Moneylenders gave back the unjust fees they had taken. Even thieves began leading honest lives. Anthony's preaching was a great success, but he was very sick. When Lent was over, the other friars convinced him to take a rest in the town of Camposampiero.

But the crowds followed him even there. There were so many people that Anthony asked the friars to build him a little tree house in the branches of a large walnut tree. Then he was able to pray and preach from the tree, always surrounded by a crowd of children and adults.

One day, after coming down from the walnut tree to eat with the brothers, Anthony felt ill. He knew it was time to go and meet the Lord in heaven. He asked to be brought back to Padua. When he died, he was only thirty-six years old.

Many statues and holy images of Anthony show him as tall and slender, with light hair. In real life, he had dark hair and was not very tall or thin. Paintings of Saint Anthony sometimes show him with a lily, which stands for his purity, and a book that is the symbol of his wisdom. Most of the time, he is holding baby Jesus in his arms. This is how Count Tiso, a friend of the friars, saw him one night when, curious to see why light was shining out of Anthony's room, he went to look.

The feast of Saint Anthony falls on June 13. Saint Anthony is a doctor of the Church and the protector of the poor and orphans. People often pray to him to help them find lost objects. Anthony's name means "priceless" or "praiseworthy."

Saint Catherine

Catherine was born in Siena, Italy, in the year 1347. She was the twenty-fourth of twenty-five children of Jacopo Benincasa and his wife, Lapa. Catherine had a twin sister who died when she was born.

Catherine was a beautiful little girl. But she was different from other children. She liked to go to church

to pray or to stay alone to meditate and to do penance, instead of playing with her friends.

When she was six years old, she saw Jesus for the first time. He was sitting on a throne wearing a white garment and the vestments of a bishop. Saints Peter and Paul were next to him. Jesus smiled at Catherine.

Jesus appeared to Catherine and spoke to her many other times, too. Jesus made her so wise that various popes later gave her the titles doctor of the Church, patron of Italy, and finally patron of all of Europe.

When Catherine was still very young, her mother wanted to find her a husband. She encouraged Catherine to wear beautiful dresses and fix her hair in a pretty way. But Catherine didn't want to get married. She shaved off all her hair and stubbornly refused to go out of the house. There was no way to make her change her mind, even with punishments. Her parents finally gave in and let Catherine follow her vocation.

At the age of sixteen, Catherine entered the Third Order of Saint Dominic. At that time, it was called the Order of the Mantellate, because the members wore a black mantle over a white habit. They lived in their own homes instead of in a convent or monastery. Catherine dedicated herself to the care of the sick, the poor, and those condemned to death. Her words brought everyone comfort and hope.

Little by little, Catherine became famous for being very holy and wise. Many people began coming to see her at her house in Siena. Catherine had never gone to school. She had only learned to read and write as an adult. Still, the intelligent and powerful men of her time came to ask Catherine what they should do. She said a prayer for everyone who came to see her. She also gave each person good advice.

Catherine wrote or, most of the time, dictated to someone, letters full of wisdom and faith. She even sent letters to kings and politicians. She wasn't afraid to tell anyone the truth. She wrote many letters to the pope, too. Because of political trouble in Rome, the popes had been living in Avignon, France, for several years. Catherine asked the pope to return to Rome because the people needed him there. But the pope wasn't sure that he should go back. So Catherine decided to go to Avignon to convince him in person. In the end,

she accomplished her mission. The pope finally returned to the city where Saint Peter had died.

Through Catherine's prayers to God, miracles happened while she was still living. One time, a woman had some old wheat that she wanted to throw away because it was moldy. "Please give me the wheat," Catherine asked her. "I want to make some bread for the poor." The woman gave Catherine the wheat, and Catherine kneaded it and put it in the oven. The bread that came out was the best that anyone had ever tasted! The woman was convinced that it was the Blessed

Mother herself who had helped Catherine make the bread.

Here's a story about another miracle: like many people in those days, Catherine's father used to make wine. He used large barrels. The wine in one of the barrels went bad. But Catherine's father wouldn't throw it away. When a poor man came to the house, Catherine didn't want to give him the bad-tasting wine to drink. So she took wine from her father's last good barrel. When the worker in charge of the wine cellar found out, he scolded her. He was afraid there wouldn't be enough wine left for the family. Instead, the barrel never ran out until the new grapes were harvested.

On April 29, 1380, Catherine died, worn out by fasting and penance. She was just thirty-three years old.

Saint Catherine is the protector of nurses and of the dying. Artists usually show her wearing a black mantle.

Some paintings show her having a vision of Jesus. Others show her caring for the sick. Her symbols are the book, the cross, and the crown of thorns. Catherine's name means "pure." Her feast day is April 29.

Saint Rita

We don't know the exact year that Rita was born. It was probably around 1386. We do know that she was born in Roccaporena, a little village near Cascia, Italy.

Rita's parents, Anthony and Amata, were already elderly when she was born. They had waited a long time for a baby. They welcomed Rita with great joy.

Anthony and Amata were peacemakers in their village. It was their job to help people reach an agreement whenever there were problems in families or in the town government. They taught young Rita how important it is to forgive others always and to live in peace.

Rita was obedient and meek. She felt attracted to the religious life. She liked to go off alone and pray. But when her parents promised her in marriage to a young man, she quietly accepted their decision.

Rita got married and had twin boys. They were named Giangiacomo and Paolo Maria. She was always busy with her children and with the housework. Unfortunately, her husband, Paolo, had a bad character. He didn't talk much and was rude. Some people also said that he was violent. In spite of all this, Rita was patient and always tried to love Paolo and be kind to him. She had to ask him for permission for anything she wanted to do—even to go to church. But little by little, her goodness began to change him.

Then a very sad thing happened. One evening, while Paolo was returning home along a path through the mountain, some men attacked and killed him. Maybe it was a robbery. Or it could have been an act of revenge for something Paolo had done in the past. Rita was heartbroken and very worried. In those days, a killing was always paid back with another killing.

Giangiacomo and Paolo Maria were already fifteen years old. Rita was afraid that they might decide to take revenge and commit a crime themselves. She prayed to God that this wouldn't happen. A short time later, the two boys died, probably due to an epidemic of sickness.

Now Rita was all alone. But her new suffering gave her the chance to set a good example to others. She went to her husband's killer and forgave him. She asked her relatives to forgive him too. They were very upset and refused to do it.

Rita didn't get discouraged. She kept trying until the members of the two families gave up hating one another

and finally asked one another for pardon. After that, many people who were quarreling with others came to Rita for advice. She always helped them to find a way to make peace.

In the meantime, Rita was trying to fulfill her dream of dedicating her life entirely to the Lord. She asked to enter the monastery of Saint Mary Magdalene in Cascia. The nuns turned her down at least three times. They may have been afraid to get involved in the tension between the two rival families. Or maybe they felt that Rita was not well educated. The nuns may also have believed that Rita would have a hard time getting used to life in the monastery because she had been married.

Whatever the reason was, a legend tells us that one night while she was praying, Rita saw Saint John the Baptist, Saint Augustine, and Saint Nicolas of Tolentino, three of her favorite saints. They called her and brought her into the monastery, over the high walls and through the locked door. After this miracle, the nuns had to welcome her into their community. Rita lived in the monastery and dedicated herself to prayer and acts of charity until the day she died after a long illness.

Rita is called the "saint of the thorns" because one Good Friday a thorn from the crown of Jesus pierced her forehead. She is also called the "saint of the roses." One winter day, while she was very ill, one of her relatives came to visit. She asked Rita if there was anything she would like. "I would like very much to have a rose," Rita said.

"A rose? That's impossible," the relative answered. "It's January, and it's too cold out!" But the next morning Rita's relative, looking out at her garden, was amazed to see a beautiful red rose that had grown during the night!

Paintings of Saint Rita show her dressed as a nun, with a thorn in her forehead. Some pictures also show her holding a book. Saint Rita has prayed to God to help people in many desperate and painful situations. This is why Saint Rita is called the "saint of the impossible." Her name means "pearl." Saint Rita's feast day is May 22.

Saint John Bosco

John Bosco was born on August 16, 1815, in Becchi, Italy. His parents were peasants. His father, Francis, died when John was only two years old. His mother, Margaret, had to raise her three children by herself.

Life at that time was very hard. Even the children had to work. As soon as John was old enough, his mother

gave him a cow to bring to pasture. He became a herder, like many of his friends.

When John was nine years old, he had a dream. In it, he saw a big house with a courtyard. Many boys were playing and laughing there. Some of them were using bad language. John held up his fists to those who were cursing. He was ready to fight with them. Just then, a man wearing a white garment appeared. His face was radiant. "Don't hit them," the man said to John. "Help them to become your friends by using goodness and charity. Explain to them that friendship with the Lord is a precious gift."

The years went by. John's mother taught him to pray and to help the poor and the sick. Then he could run and play with the other boys. And John loved to play! He was always the winner when his friends had a race. He knew how to walk on a tightrope like an acrobat. He could juggle, too. John was also a great storyteller. Other children always came to listen to him and watch his "performances." Before John put on a show, however, everyone had to recite a prayer. He never let anyone use bad language, either.

John seemed to be living out the dream he had once had. But he wanted to do much more. He wanted to become a priest. In order to do that, though, he needed to go to school. Unfortunately, schools were expensive. His mother couldn't afford the fees.

But thanks to his determination and the help of many good people, John was able to study for the priesthood. First some priests gave him lessons. Then John entered the seminary. To support himself and pay the fees, he worked as he studied. He worked in the stables, cleaned the house, did tailoring jobs, and was even a waiter. All these experiences would help him in special ways later on.

On June 5, 1841, John was ordained a priest in Turin, Italy. He was placed under the guidance of Father Cafasso, who prepared the young priests for the work they would do.

The Industrial Revolution had brought many people from the countryside to the big city of Turin to find work in the factories. The workday was long, but the people were paid very little. Even children had to work

to help feed their families. Young boys, only eight or ten years old, waited in the city streets for someone to bring them to the mills or construction sites. They worked there as chimneysweepers. Some no longer had their parents.

Father Bosco began taking care of these boys. He gathered them together by holding contests, playing games, and letting them have fun in a place he called the Oratory. First, Father Bosco would celebrate Mass for the boys, and then he'd give them something to eat. The number of boys who came to enjoy themselves, to pray, and to find a place to sleep kept growing. Sadly, Father Bosco and the boys were evicted from the property. Father Bosco had to find another house for them all.

Father Bosco named his new Oratory after Saint Francis de Sales. After this first Oratory, Father Bosco began others. He wanted his boys to learn how to read and write. He wanted them to learn a trade. Father Bosco knew that if the boys learned different skills, they could save themselves from poverty and home-lessness. Remembering all the experiences he had had as a young worker, Father Bosco started workshops where boys were taught to become shoemakers, tailors, carpenters, locksmiths, and printers. Father Bosco's mother came to Turin to help him to care for the poor boys he took in. She cooked, washed, and mended their ragged clothes.

Little by little, many priests and lay people came to help Father Bosco. Soon he began a new religious congregation of priests and brothers. Later, with the help of Mary Mazzarello (who also became a saint), he began a congregation of sisters to educate young girls. These congregations, together with the laypeople who help them, make up the Salesian Family, which is dedicated to the education and care of young people. In 1875, the first Salesians left Italy for South America. Today there are Salesians doing God's work all over the world. When Father John Bosco died, on January 31, 1888, there were hundreds of workshops, professional schools, houses, and colleges all following his educational method.

Saint John Bosco is the protector of teachers, students, and those who are learning a trade. His feast day falls on January 31. The name John means "God is merciful" or "gift of God."

Saint Bernadette

Bernadette Soubirous was born on January 7, 1844, in the town of Lourdes, France. Her family lived in an old mill, which her father, François, and her mother, Louise, had rented. Life in those days was hard and tiresome for the workers and the farmers of that area. Bernadette's family was one of the poorest in the town. Because he had many debts that he couldn't pay, François Soubirous eventually had to give up his job of running the mill. He went to work as a hired hand to support his four children. Bernadette's family had to move into a damp and cold building. It had once been a prison. Not only that, but Mr. Soubirous was falsely accused of stealing some flour. He was arrested and sent to jail for a short time.

To earn money for the family, Mrs. Soubirous went to do washing in the homes of wealthy families. Bernadette also went to work as a shepherdess at the farm of a family friend. She lived with this family for a while.

One day, after she was back at home again, Bernadette went with her sister Toinette and their friend Jeanne to gather wood for their fireplace. It was February 11, 1858, and Bernadette was fourteen years old. To get to a spot where they could find some tree branches, they had to cross a small stream flowing from the Gave River. Bernadette had asthma, and the water was freezing. Toinette and Jeanne took off their stockings.

They squealed loudly as they ran through the ice-cold water.

Bernadette tried to find rocks to step on so she could cross over without getting her feet wet. But it was useless. As she started to take off her stockings to wade across, a gust of wind caught her attention. She looked up at the grotto formed by a large rock at the edge of the river. The place was called Massabielle. She was amazed to see a beautiful young Lady standing in the opening of the rock. The Lady wore a long white dress with a blue waistband. There was a yellow rose on each of her feet. She held a rosary in her hands. The Lady smiled at Bernadette.

Bernadette couldn't believe what she was seeing. She rubbed her eyes. But when she looked again, the apparition was still there! Bernadette tried to make the sign of the cross, but her arm fell down. She finally pulled her rosary from her pocket. The Lady began passing the beads of her own rosary through her fingers without moving her lips. Bernadette tried again and was able to make the sign of the cross and pray the Rosary. After that, the Lady vanished.

This was the first of eighteen apparitions, during which the Lady asked Bernadette to do penance for sinners and to pray. The Lady also asked to have a chapel built at the grotto and to have people go there in processions.

Soon word spread that the Blessed Mother had appeared to Bernadette. At first everyone just laughed. Why would Mary appear to a poor and ignorant girl who couldn't even read or write?

At first, not even Bernadette's parents believed her. They told her not to go back to the grotto. But Bernadette was courageous. She returned every time the Lady called her. Some curious people started to go with her. At first, there were only a few. Soon, however, the crowds grew bigger and bigger. On Sunday, February 28, there were 2,000 people at the grotto. Now many of the people believed Bernadette. Witnesses have written that when Bernadette saw the Lady, her face was transformed. She looked perfectly happy and her eyes were radiant with light. Not even the flame of a candle touching her hand distracted her from her ecstasy or burned her fingers.

Even the newspapers began to report these facts. The government authorities wanted an investigation of the events at the grotto. An imperial procurator questioned Bernadette. Her parish priest listened cautiously to Bernadette's account. A doctor wrote down what happened to her during the apparitions. Everyone wanted to know for sure who this Lady dressed in white really was.

Bernadette asked the Lady her name more than once. But the Lady only answered her on March 25. She said, "I am the Immaculate Conception." Bernadette didn't understand what this meant. She ran to tell her pastor. When he heard these words, he was speechless. He knew then that Bernadette had really seen the Blessed Mother!

During one of the apparitions, the beautiful Lady asked Bernadette to drink the water below the rock. When she couldn't find any water, Bernadette dug in the mud with her hands. Afterward, a spring began to flow at that spot. From that day until now, about ninety people have been miraculously cured by using this Lourdes water.

To escape all the attention that the apparitions brought her, Bernadette went to live at a convent. There she learned how to read and to write. Later, she became a sister herself. She was very sick with asthma and tuberculosis, but she spent her short life helping the other sick sisters in the infirmary of the convent. She was only thirty-five years old when she died.

Bernadette's name means "the little one who is as brave as a bear." She is the patron of Lourdes, France, and the holy protector of the sick. Her feast day is April 16.

The Archangel Gabriel

The Archangel Gabriel is the angel whom God sent to ask Mary to become the Mother of Jesus. Gabriel is considered a messenger of God not only by Christians, but also by Jews and Muslims.

Angels are beings that join the earth with heaven. They are heavenly creatures who take on a human form

in order to carry messages from God to people on earth. Angels become visible and speak and act as if they were human beings. Sometimes they look like travelers. Certain angels have appeared as older persons. Others look like strong young men. In the Bible, angels often come to people in their dreams. The Sacred Scriptures are full of stories of angels who protect, heal, teach, reveal, sing, and praise God. Each one of them has a special duty.

Gabriel's duty is to announce the wonderful birth of babies who are destined to change the history of humanity. The Gospel of Luke tells us that the Angel Gabriel was sent by God to a village of Galilee called Nazareth to a virgin named Mary. Gabriel entered her house and said, "Hail Mary, full of grace, the Lord is with you."

When Mary saw Gabriel and heard these words, she didn't know what to think. She couldn't understand what the angel's greeting meant.

Then Gabriel continued. "You will give birth to a son and you will call him Jesus. This baby that is to be born from you will be holy and will be called the Son of God.

Elizabeth, your relative who was not able to have a baby, is also going to have a son."

Gabriel brought not only the message of the birth of Jesus, but also that of John the Baptist. In fact, before visiting Mary, Gabriel had already appeared to Zechariah, Elizabeth's husband. He brought Zechariah joyful news. "Do not be afraid, Zechariah," Gabriel said. "God has heard your prayer. Your wife Elizabeth will give you a son whom you will call John. I am Gabriel, and I stand before the presence of God. I have been sent to speak to you and to bring you this good news."

Because Gabriel has appeared in events that involve babies, he is the protector of unborn babies and infants.

There are many popular stories and legends about angels coming from heaven to help people. In Sardinia, Italy, there is a cove called the Gulf of the Angels. It's named after an ancient legend. The legend says that one day the angels asked God if they could go and live on earth. God said yes, so all the angels left heaven to look for a peaceful and happy place on earth. They

quickly discovered that everywhere they looked on earth there was nothing but fighting and hatred. They were almost ready to give up and return to heaven when they came across a beautiful land near the sea.

It really seemed to be a corner of paradise, and the people who lived there were gentle and hardworking. So the angels decided that is where they wanted to live. Now as soon as the devil saw them, he was envious. He rushed to that place and tried to make the angels leave.

A great battle followed between the angels and the devil. Even the waves of the sea rose up high. Finally, the Archangel Gabriel triumphantly came out of the waves holding his sword of light. The devil was furious at having been bounced off his black horse. He threw his saddle at one of the hills with all his might. Even today, that hill has the shape of a horse's saddle.

Many paintings of the Archangel Gabriel show him as a young man with wings and a white robe. His symbol is the lily, which he gave to Mary at the Annunciation. Gabriel's name means "man of God."

Besides being the protector of little babies, Saint Gabriel is also the patron saint of all who work in the world of communication and in the spreading of news through television, radio, and newspapers. His feast day is September 29, together with the Archangels Michael and Raphael.

Who are the Daughters of St. Paul?

We are Catholic sisters. Our mission is to be like Saint Paul and tell everyone about Jesus! There are so many ways for people to communicate with each other. We want to use all of them so everyone will know how much God loves us. We do this by printing books (you're holding one!), making radio shows, singing, helping people at our bookstores, using the Internet, and in many other ways.

Visit our Web site at www.pauline.org

Pauline
BOOKS & MEDIA

The Daughters of St. Paul operate book and media centers at the following addresses. Visit, call or write the one nearest you today, or find us on the World Wide Web, www.pauline.org.

CALIFORNIA
3908 Sepulveda Blvd, Culver City, CA 90230   310-397-8676
2640 Broadway Street, Redwood City, CA 94063   650-369-4230
5945 Balboa Avenue, San Diego, CA 92111   858-565-9181

FLORIDA
145 S.W. 107th Avenue, Miami, FL 33174   305-559-6715

HAWAII
1143 Bishop Street, Honolulu, HI 96813   808-521-2731

Neighbor Islands call: 866-521-2731

ILLINOIS
172 North Michigan Avenue, Chicago, IL 60601   312-346-4228

LOUISIANA
4403 Veterans Memorial Blvd, Metairie, LA 70006   504-887-7631

MASSACHUSETTS
885 Providence Hwy, Dedham, MA 02026   781-326-5385

MISSOURI
9804 Watson Road, St. Louis, MO 63126   314 965 3512

NEW YORK
64 West 38th Street, New York, NY 10018   212-754-1110

PENNSYLVANIA
9171-A Roosevelt Blvd, Philadelphia, PA 19114   215-676-9494

SOUTH CAROLINA
243 King Street, Charleston, SC 29401   843-577-0175

VIRGINIA
1025 King Street, Alexandria, VA 22314   703-549-3806

CANADA
3022 Dufferin Street, Toronto, ON M6B 3T5   416-781-9131